Francis Knights

Studying music without going to university:

An alternative education

Peacock Press

Studying music without going to university: An alternative education
Copyright © 2022 Francis Knights

ISBN 978-1-914934-35-3

Published by Peacock Press, 2022
Scout Bottom Farm
Mytholmroyd
Hebden Bridge HX7 5JS (UK)

Design and artwork by DM Design and Print
Cover photograph: Francis Knights

Francis Knights

Studying music without going to university:

An alternative education

Foreword

The expansion of the British higher education system over the past 30 years, and the subsequent introduction of high fees, with student loans to help cover them, has changed the educational landscape in many ways. In the past few years, serious concerns about affordability, access and course content have become part of widespread and sometimes heated public debate.[1] The humanities have been particularly impacted, as students, universities, employers and governments[2] all weigh the long-term financial or status value of certain degrees against others, with each doing so from their own sometimes-incompatible perspectives. Music is one subject that has particularly suffered in respect of declining numbers, and the proposal offered here explores one possible alternative to the traditional three-year full-time residential undergraduate degree, with a primary focus on the structure and quality of the education itself, rather than the accreditation processes which are currently regarded as providing much of the economic justification for university study.

The specific remit adopted below is for the traditional study of classical music in England, although the system outlined is designed to be sufficiently flexible that it could easily be adapted for other academic environments (for example, a conservatoire-type approach would greatly increase the proportion of practical music) or countries, or for the specialist study of any other musical style, such as jazz, pop or folk. In addition, it could even be reconfigured for other comparable humanities subjects such as Art and Modern languages[3] – both of which have critical practical components that can be very effectively taught on a one-to-one basis – and perhaps even for the study of Classics, Philosophy, English or History.

The structure of this book outlines the historical basis for musical study before it was a formal part of the university curriculum, then looks at what might now be taught privately and how it might best be taught, with a view to providing a flexible, affordable alternative

---

1   For one recent contribution to the debate, which argues for more flexibility within the university sector, see Rees (2021); see also Collini (2017). Adult education issues are discussed in the Centenary Commission on Adult Education report https://www.centenarycommission.org, among others, while small new institutions such as the New Model Institute of Technology and Engineering, https://nmite.ac.uk or the London Interdisciplinary School, https://www.lis.ac.uk, demonstrate innovative approaches within the university system, the value of which time will tell.

2   Similarly, the national funding of arts research has skewed such research activity for many years; for a survey see Summers (2007).

3   Languages are another subject for which there is some external certification of competence available.

educational system. There are both advantages and disadvantages to this method, and every attempt is made to lay out these issues fairly, in order that prospective students understand both the benefits and the potential challenges of going it alone.

Francis Knights
Cambridge
February 2022

CONTENTS

1. Introduction

The high standard cost of a university degree in music in England – average student debt for 2020 graduates was £45,000 – coupled with the subject's low relative Graduate Premium (the earnings uplift resulting from a degree qualification)[4] means that such study has become less appealing in recent years, which is reflected by the precipitous decline in A-level music numbers,[5] an indicator of future degree subject interest. In addition, the perception remains that classical music is an 'elite' subject (despite the fact that, through film, television and radio, music from Western classical traditions is actually being heard by more people than at any time in its history), and therefore of less 'relevance' or interest to those from other social backgrounds or classes. This study examines the history of the academic music degree, and looks at the existing and future possibilities for flexible and more affordable alternatives.

Although differential fee structures (for example, higher charges for students outside the home country, for the same course) have a long history, many countries operate financial subject equivalency; that is, whatever the actual cost of delivering a degree-course structure (far greater for medicine than history, for example), annual fees charged to the student or funding body are the same. However, this is beginning to change in some countries, and in a reverse direction that might be expected: subjects that are cheaper to deliver are being charged more, as a result of government desires to encourage subjects seen as of national economic benefit, such as science and technology, by discouraging those seen as of less value. The process is already underway in Australia, where it has led to significant rises in fees for arts subjects. In the UK, fears of this kind have been raised by a Consultation on Recurrent Funding,[6] which could propose further reductions in funding for arts subjects, perhaps leading to differential fees. Music is not well placed in this respect: compared to other humanities studies, it is relatively expensive to deliver at degree level, as it includes an unusually large set of both resources and skills, undertaken individually and in ensemble.

This study explores concerns about the impact of the present high cost of a university degree in music on the future of the subject, and is given additional topicality by recent events involving Brexit and the Covid pandemic, both of which look to seriously harm the

---

4   Britton et al. (2020).

5   The numbers halved between 2008-2020; Joint Council for Qualifications,
    at https://analytics.ofqual.gov.uk/apps/Alevel/Outcomes.

6   https://www.officeforstudents.org.uk.

financial viability of classical music careers in Britain. This is highly likely to have the result of drawing yet more potential students away from studying the subject, and in particular reinforce the notion that a career in classical music is only open to those with the family resources to sustain it.[7] How serious study of the subject, at each of undergraduate, Master's and PhD level, can be undertaken by those with more limited resources may depend on some students moving away from the traditional full-time funded-study pattern, and such options are examined here.

The recent 'professionalization' and subsequent gathering of nearly all music research activities into university and conservatoire settings may also have led to a narrowing of potential focus, as Ronald Hutton observes with respect to archaeology.[8] For example, of the 30 articles published by *Early Music* in 2020, a leading journal founded with a broad readership remit and which still has an unusually high number of private subscribers, 26 are by academics and the remaining four by well-established independent scholars of a very similar kind.

The scope of the discussion here is deliberately restricted to one particular case – the study of Western art music ('classical music') in England,[9] although there will of course be parallels with the educational and financial arrangements in other places, and equivalent study course descriptions could be created to cover a wide variety of musical styles. Nevertheless, the particular problem to be addressed here is only relevant to places where there are few alternatives to expensive degree structures.

Study abroad was formerly an economical option, with a number of European institutions offering English-language tuition at rates far below those of England, but post-Brexit, UK students are now subject to international fees similar in size to those in England.[10] The generous but highly competitive international scholarship schemes offered by some US universities represent another potential route.

---

7   The same concern has been raised in respect to training as an actor, as shown in Friedman, Laurison and Miles (2015); it is now largely a middle class profession. In addition, high-quality secondary-level music provision is becoming the preserve of private schools; see Bath et al. (2020).

8   Hutton (2013), pp.135ff.

9   University application arrangements for Wales, Northern Ireland and Scotland are all handled by https://www.ucas.com, but the loan-funding arrangements for the first two (https://www.gov.uk/government/organisations/student-loans-company) differ from the latter (https://www.mygov.scot/apply-student-loan).

10 For a list, see https://www.educations.com; an example is the Conservatorium Maastricht https://www.conservatoriummaastricht.nl.

2. A History of Music Education

Music degrees in composition in England have a very ancient history, having been awarded since at least 1463 (Cambridge) and 1499 (Oxford).[11] These were non-residential, and in effect awarded on the basis of a substantial submitted composition demonstrating a high level of professional expertise (for example, the highly complex polyphonic *Missa O quam glorifica* composed by Robert Fayrfax, 1504).[12] In due course, a performance of the work was required in addition, and a period of study specified – for example, seven years for a BMus and a further five for a DMus – without defining exactly what was to be studied, how or with whom.[13] The professional certification offered by these non-residential degrees made them popular with practising musicians from the middle of the 16th century onwards, and graduates included Amner, Bull, Dowland, Farnaby, Gibbons, Loosemore, Morley, Mundy, Peerson, Ramsey, Ravenscroft, Tomkins, Tye, Weelkes, White and many others.[14]

Academic degrees in music in Britain are a relatively recent innovation, dating from just after the Second World War. Before that, the subject was seen essentially as practical, even if (for example) music theory and history became subjects of increasing interest to Oxford (and especially Edinburgh) professors of music from the 19th century onwards.[15] In Britain, previous extended works of theory over the centuries had usually emerged from practitioners (for example, Thomas Morley's *A plaine and easie introduction to practicall musicke* (1597)

---

11 Williams (1893), Carpenter (1955), Cudworth (1964) and Dart (1964).

12 Some examined essay content was added by Oxford from 1858, and the performance requirement not abolished there until 1891; see Golding (2013), pp.72, 86.

13 Interestingly, references to Boethius (d.524) and his derivative *De Institutione Musica* (Kárpáti (1987)) did not disappear from Oxford until the middle of the 19th century, a reflection of the dominance of Classics at Oxford and Cambridge until then. While music was a Quadrivium topic during the Middle Ages, it had no Faculty of its own: in medieval Cambridge, for the 'systematic academic study of music there is no evidence whatever'; Leedham-Green (1996), p.18.

14 Williams (1893).

15 For a history of the long and complex transition process from non-residential composition degrees to academic music degrees, see Golding (2013) and Golding (2018). Some interesting general historical insights can also be gleaned by examining one group whose studies perforce had to occur outside the universities: women. See Riley (2017), ch.2 'Educating a Lady'.

or Christopher Simpson's *A Compendium of Practical Musick* (1667))[16] on a 'how-to' basis, but from about 1800 performer-scholars with a more musicological interest in their subject (William Crotch, *Specimens of Various Styles of Music* ([1808-1810]) and *Elements of Musical Composition* (1812),[17] John Stainer, *The Music of the Bible* (1879)) began to contribute to the academic and pedagogical development of the subject, and demand for textbooks[18] (for example, the very large number of works on fugue published from the early 19th century onwards)[19] was stimulated by the creation of music conservatoires – including the Royal Academy of Music (founded 1822) and Royal College of Music (founded 1882)[20] in London – and thereafter by the explosion in the number of universities in the 20th century.[21] Inspired by his Italian travels, Charles Burney had in the 18th century proposed the creation of a conservatoire in Britain, but it came to nothing.[22] It was actually the widespread adoption of degree-awarding powers in the post-war period that created uniformity across the sector; before that, individual and highly-respected institutional diplomas and other awards (such as Associate of the Royal Academy of Music or Fellowship of the Royal College of Organists) provided a form of academic equivalence for the discipline.

With such academic qualifications came structured courses, but of course musicians have always studied their subject privately through such courses,[23] whether it was Tallis teaching Byrd imitative counterpoint, Mozart setting minuets for Thomas Attwood[24] or Herbert Brewer at Gloucester Cathedral teaching the young Herbert Howells.[25] On the continent, certain 18th-century teachers and theorists achieved international fame through their work, such as Padre Martini (1706-1784) and Johann Joseph Fux (c.1660-1741).

---

16 Even amateurs contributed substantial books, such as Charles Butler's *The Principles of Musik, in Singing and Setting* (1636); see Pruett (1963).

17 Crotch (1812) is a remarkable all-in-one study guide, which is still in print (facsimile, Cambridge University Press, 2013) and usable today.

18 For a useful guide to the development of such books since the Tudor period, see Rainbow (2009).

19 See Francis Knights, 'A history of fugue teaching in Britain' (forthcoming).

20 As well as the 18th century Italian institutions, these were also preceded by conservatoires at Paris (1795), Prague (1811), Graz (1815) and Vienna (1817).

21 Anderson (2006).

22 Kassler (1972).

23 Necessarily with the restricted syllabus relevant to their area of activity.

24 Heartz (1973-1974).

25 Brewer (2015).

The system of Articled Pupils operated by Brewer and his predecessors and contemporaries within the English cathedral tradition is especially worthy of note, as it offered a form of private, direct and intensive study at a time before suitable university courses existed.[26] For example, Herbert Sumsion (1899-1995) undertook a three-year apprenticeship in organ, choral direction and music theory with Brewer, culminating in the FRCO diploma; he eventually succeeded his teacher at Gloucester Cathedral.

---

26 It could be argued that the postwar undergraduate music syllabus emerged partly from the model of the Royal College of Organists' diplomas, which still involve performance, keyboard skills, aural, history essays, and harmony and counterpoint exercises; see https://www.rco.org.uk/examinations_qualifications.php.

3. Undergraduate-level courses

Private academic study

Part-time options for specialist or research study of music at postgraduate level are well established, but the choices for first degrees – the initial and most critical period of formal academic training – are much more problematic.[27] Such education is intrinsically expensive, and institutional finances, even degree course design, are predicated on the systems of state funding (in the case of England, via student loans) currently in place.[28] Student numbers themselves are critical for continued viability, creating a marketized system. In effect, therefore, the incentives for a lower-cost system do not exist: the ability to confer a degree is the intrinsic economic power of a university. Because of this, the first-degree alternatives discussed below are necessarily radical, and are complicated by the fact that other accreditation systems themselves offer only partial alternatives at undergraduate level.[29]

The model proposed is based on historical examples, and in effect repurposes some of the funds that would otherwise be spent on a formal undergraduate degree programme, in order to 'buy' the equivalent specialist teaching direct from experts, in the same way that practical music lessons are organized. There is a great deal of beneficial flexibility possible, and courses could be designed either on the traditional university (academic) or conservatoire (practical) model, depending on student requirements. It comes at far lower cost, without the necessity to support a university's high-cost buildings, administrators, infrastructure, libraries, support services, pensions and so forth, and the fundamental question is whether a student can be given privately a comparable structured course of study where the loss of such facilities does not impact too severely on the quality of teaching and its processes.

---

27 The Open University offers a distance-learning music BA either full- or part-time, at rates amounting to two-thirds of the normal university fee in England; see http://www.open.ac.uk.

28 Fees are normally around £9,000 pa, to which substantial living costs must be added.

29 A great deal of research has been undertaken concerning undergraduate-level music pedagogy, curriculum design and so forth, especially in the US, but almost all researchers assume the university and conservatory are the only medium of education delivery. Even a recent proposal with the promising title 'Transforming Music Study from Its Foundations', by Campbell et al. (2016), does not think outside this institutional framework.

The Course Director

The essential feature of this model is an expert 'lead' teacher or Course Director, who can design a structured degree-level programme to be delivered over a period of three or four years, which both enables to student to cover the key areas of the subject and allows later specialist exploration (see Chapter 4). In other words, a real equivalent to a normal degree programme, and with a high number of direct contact hours. It is desirable that this should involve a traditional course-based, term-like structure, in order to lay out each complete year's progression and rate of work, following sequential years of study where the skills and standards required are continually rising.[30] Such a teacher would actually perform the role of a college Director of Studies within the current Cambridge University system: providing the principal direct teaching, offering overall academic guidance and arranging the additional tutors. The flexible nature of the system would allow additional specialist teaching to be bought in (sometimes remotely, where necessary) for certain subjects. Similarly, teacher-set examinations (which would be important as a term- or year-end personal goals for each course, rather than any way of comparing students with each other) could also be marked externally and at cost, by way of outside validation for the student.

The administrative skills and personality of the Course Director are critical: the student must trust that the material is appropriate, and that the tutors appointed are both expert and motivated. In order to get the best out of the system, the Director and student should agree at the beginning of each year on the length, timing and frequency of teaching for each course (individual tutorials could each be timed at 30' or 60' as appropriate); the expectation of both sides in terms of workload and examinations; and the fee structure (see below). In other words, a real equivalent of a university course structure: anything less is likely to lead to ambiguity, casualness and consequent dissatisfaction. Critically, one-to-one academic relationships of this kind require *both* sides to be organized, efficient and committed, especially because there could be no actual sanctions or penalties for either side choosing to discontinue the teaching or learning at any time. A simple but formal quasi-contractual written arrangement is likely to provide the best educational superstructure to enable continuity and support. In particular, pre-Tutorial preparation in terms of reading or other tasks needs to be clearly formalized as an essential activity, in the absence of traditional university lectures.

----

30 It is important that any bespoke course covers the basics (history, analysis, harmony and counterpoint and so on) in sufficient detail; professional musical activity takes many forms, but the fundamental skills and understanding such activity relies on are always transferable.

Scaling the system

This model should function very well in ideal circumstances for a single student, but there are real economies of scale available if several students study together in this way. This would also has the advantage of creating a small academic peer group, which is otherwise lacking. This is in effect reconstituting something of the old Articled Pupil model described above. While recent experience with delivering remote learning during the Covid pandemic has proved the utility of some online approaches,[31] it is in no way suitable or desirable for a complete programme of musical study: there is real value in personal contact and support. Built interpersonal relationships of trust would be essential for studies to progress well over a period of years. Ideally, frequent in-person contact with the Course Director would maintain the pace of progress, and support motivation; in addition, frequent feedback means that the teaching could be very precisely tailored to the student's strengths, and weaknesses.

It would be ideal if all course teaching and practical instruction (including instrumental and vocal lessons) were in person as far as possible, and this means a location with sufficient capable teachers, probably meaning a city rather than a small town. A larger place would also have more musicians to interact with, more concerts to attend, more performing opportunities, better physical library resources and so on. In the absence of a student year-group, it would be vital for a private student to participate fully in local choirs, orchestras and so on, as a great deal of musical learning and consolidation occurs in such environments. It is unfortunate that the places where there is a large pool of retired senior music academics and under-employed junior academics who do not yet have permanent university roles – many of whom would make excellent Course Directors – available for such private degree-level teaching (Oxford, Cambridge, York, Durham and a number of large cities) are also among the most expensive places in the country to live.[32] It should be noted that there are also a number of private music teachers who would be well capable of delivering this level and quality of teaching.[33]

---

31 The distance learning of music is by no means a modern invention; for example, Bruckner's harmony lessons with Simon Sechter in 1855-1861 were by post; see Hawkshaw (2007).

32 The extent to which a student could fund travel from their home to such a place, probably several times a week, would be part of an overall costing plan.

33 For recent research as to the work of private music teachers, see Barton (2019).

Library resources

One major cost of the traditional residential system is the provision of library and other resources, and these are challenging to access privately. Where geographically accessible, major public libraries are one possible resource,[34] and some academic libraries allow access (if not borrowing) by individual arrangement. While online score resources are excellent for Public Domain works, access to copyright material such as modern music, research articles (via JSTOR for example, see Appendix) and books would be an issue for a non-institutional student, and may even constrain exactly what can be studied.[35] However, some second-hand mainstream material such as books is not hard to find cheaply, and the private student would need to make creating their own library collection a primary task, as it was in the past.

Online teaching resources

The one-to-one tutorial relationship described above is particularly suitable for regular set exercises (essays, harmony exercises and so on), but some of the more lecture-like content could also be provided elsewhere. Fortunately, there is a certain amount of good material now available online via some MOOCs,[36] and this could be supplemented with other public lectures (for example, those offered by Gresham College in London),[37] conference attendance, summer schools and so on, costs permitting. Such lectures could form the basis of a single taught course, or be blended to cover wider periods or themes. As with all electronic resources, the question is less *what* material is available than *how* an individual student can fruitfully engage with it: watching an online lecture or attending an in-person lecture are two very different experiences.

For certain repertoires or styles, studies of additional subjects such as languages, paleography, social history or physics might be appropriate, and could be built into the syllabus of Chapter 4.[38]

---

34 For example, the British Library, https://www.bl.uk: 'Undergraduate and postgraduate students are a key audience for our collections and services'.

35 See the Appendix for an introductory list of useful material.

36 Massive Open Online Courses; see https://www.my-mooc.com/en/categorie/music. Some of these are fee-based and delivered by acknowledged experts, but all tend to be introductory in style, and of less use past the first undergraduate-year equivalent. 46 different courses are offered by Berklee College of Music, for example https://www.berklee.edu/academics/moocs. Information about fees is not always easy to find.

37 https://www.gresham.ac.uk. Some universities also make their research seminars open, or put them online.

38 Similarly, the pop singer-songwriter will probably want to undertake a separate creative writing study of poetry for the purposes of writing lyrics.

Costs and fees

The critical costings for such a private course of study might be a third of a formal degree course. Apart from the hourly-rate contact teaching, agreement would be need to be made for some costs of course design and management by the Course Director, and other items such as external examination marking. Aside from the fee-cost savings, the non-residential private student – who might either being living in the family home, or be in part-time employment and resident in a house or shared house of their own[39] – could also make considerable university residence cost savings.

Fees can easily become a bone of contention, as indeed they are in the formal university system, if a student feels they are not getting value for money in terms of in-person teaching hours. Therefore, decisions on appropriate teaching rates might best be made on the basis of standard data like that collected by the Incorporated Society of Musicians;[40] hourly rates for small groups would be adjusted to share the teaching cost, one of several potential benefits of such study collaboration. Cancellation and rescheduling policies can also be borrowed from such sources, so that both student and teacher have a workable system to agree to in advance.

Self-study

Finally, it is worth thinking about whether any aspects of such a course might be studied alone, either for economy or convenience. This is a challenge in itself in terms of the learning process,[41] and even if the student is motivated enough to consistently and systematically cover a particular subject over a period of time, opportunities for discussion of the issues arising are absent, as is the invaluable feedback that marked work provides. Nevertheless, it would be possible to use a specific textbook of an appropriate type (for example, Dale, Jacob and Anson's *Harmony, Counterpoint & Improvisation*, Kraft's *Gradus* or Benjamin's *The Craft of Tonal Counterpoint*) and gain much of value from the experience.

---

39 In these instances, practice and study space may be problematic and other arrangements would need to be made.

40 https://www.ism.org.

41 As can be seen from any list of publications on autodidacticism, there are many method-advocates for self-study, but rather less research on its actual effectiveness in different circumstances. Baum (1958) reports on one study related to undergraduate mathematics students, while a new technical study by Zendel and Alexander (2020) looks at auditory development.

4. A Model Syllabus

What musical repertoire ought to be studied, and how it should be studied,[42] have become increasingly contentious questions in recent years, with tensions arising between long-established educational traditions, the needs and expectations of the profession, and newly politicized social ideals. Matthew Arnold's belief that the understanding of culture (and by extension, the purpose of education) should be done through study of 'the best which has been thought and said'[43] is regarded by some as both outdated and idealistic, with the *who* did something or *why* they did it now having become more important than *what* that something actually was. Post-modern thinking even has issues with the concept of 'quality' itself, but the music student still needs to understand what that notion might actually mean in terms of musical compositions: some pieces of music simply *are* better than others. Regardless of new societal and other external influences on the music syllabus, there has always been a three-way tension which needs resolution in designing a programme of study, and this is even more so when a bespoke syllabus is created for each student or group of students.

First, at undergraduate level the subject needs to be covered in enough breadth *and* depth to allow for the acquisition of all the skills that comprise a fully-rounded 'musician', and one that will be capable of engaging with the many different aspects of the portfolio-type career that is typical of the profession.[44] Second, the student will – but inevitably not from the point of view of a knowledgeable overview of their own – have views on what they wish (and do not wish) to study, which can all too easily correlate closely with the areas where their skills are already developed, or their natural abilities are most evident: few people like to study things they find difficult, but there are many necessary and important cases of

---

42 The desire to create a model or ideal syllabus has a long and fascinating history; see as one example that of Anton Stadler (1800), as discussed in Hess (1962/63) and Poulin (1990). Outside music, there are even examples which outline an alternative to unsatisfactory statutory provision *within* a university, such as 'Directions for a Student in the Universitie' by Richard Holdsworth, an early 17th-century Fellow of St John's College, Cambridge; see Curtis (1959), pp.108-113, 131-134, 289-290.

43 Arnold (1869), p.xi. For the Victorian background, see Newman (1852), Rothblatt (1997) and Carson (1999).

44 The essential skill sets for musicians in other traditions may be very different, for example involving significant improvisation, playing by ear, ornamentation and memorization, or the ability to work from notational shorthand such as chord symbols.

this in music. Third, the teacher will have views as to which elements and approaches are most valuable, based on their own training, pedagogical experience and wider observation. The starting point for decisions on a syllabus therefore might therefore be a negotiated agreement between teacher and student, to decide (possibly on a simple year-by-year basis) exactly what is to be covered, how *and* why.

Each stylistic discipline of musical study – classical, pop, jazz, folk, world and so on - requires its own approach and content,[45] but as it is not possible to outline a model syllabus for every one of these, let alone all their own national or stylistic sub-disciplines, what is presented here is one example of the most formal model of classical musical study, together with an explanation of what has been selected, and why. This type of rigorous, systematic and traditional course is on the decline in English universities, but still has great merits in respect of its focus on the fundamentals of musical knowledge and understanding, its deep historical grounding, and its clear progression from the general to the specific. As presented below, it is just a sample layout, to be undertaken on the basis of three full-time years of study. Of course, the content could be covered through part-time work over a longer period; or one section selected as an independent diploma-type course; and the student may not wish to progress to the subsequent year, or to change the focus of study completely. Nevertheless, experience suggests that serious coverage of any academic discipline requires the equivalent of three full-time years of concentrated work; and indeed four might well be preferable.

This syllabus is also predicated on a student of recent post-school age, or relatively early in their career. However, there are many other types of student (as the Open University's own student body shows), such as the retired, the career-changer and so on, and each of these will have different needs, as will the mature student who (for example) has decades of playing experience but wishes specifically to enhance their academic understanding of the subject.

The annual structure includes five or six courses (experience shows this to be an optimal number), most of which will run in tandem. For example, fundamentals such as Harmony

---

45 The idea that wider musical commonalities might be integrated is an obvious one (a course 'where jazz, popular, global, and classical European practices and materials are integrated with studies of improvisation, composition, rhythm, and skill development'; Campbell, Myers and Sarath (2016), p.14) but their actual employment is highly problematic, as generalized studies inevitably take time from or supplant particular repertoire studies. Student musical interests, more so than in History, English or Art, can be remarkably repertoire- and genre-specific.

and counterpoint, Analysis, Music History and Practical Music at 1st-year level contain so much material that they are best each dealt with weekly or fortnightly. Other courses, and those in the subsequent years, might work in individual termly units, or have only two or three tutorials per term (for example, dissertations or composition). Regardless, the student needs to attend each tutorial meeting after having been *set*, and *done*, a specific task, whether it be learning a piece of music, working through a harmony or analysis exercise, or writing an essay. The learning largely occurs by doing such work, and the previous tutorial represents an opportunity to explain the task, the methods and the goals, and the subsequent one to give specific feedback on the result. Every task should result in an improvement in the student's skills and understanding, and the writing of (for example) frequent – rather than occasional – essays will pay major dividends in terms of clarity of thought, expression and understanding. With each course, a clear workload needs to be assigned, so that the student can plan their annual study timetable, especially if working part-time.

First Year courses (I)

The first year includes six courses, with one optional addition (shown in italics) if required. Given the very variable quality and quantity of school music education, emphasis is on the fundamentals that are covered by all six courses, in order to provide a solid intellectual and technical foundation. The repertoire aspect of Course 1 is especially important, and structured listening tasks (with and without scores) needs to be built into this, and linked to the historical introduction of Course 4. The periods of technical study for Courses 2-5 cover the Renaissance to the Romantic, as these remain the key areas of historical repertoire for a beginning student of classical music.

1. Introduction to the study of music. Repertoire, study skills and essay writing, libraries and resources, music as communication, the musical canon, music aesthetics
2. Harmony and counterpoint. 16th to 18th century, with practical harmony at the keyboard
3. Music Analysis. An introduction to form and style, 16th to 19th century
4. Music History. Survey course from the 12th to the 21st centuries[46]
5. Practical Music. Aural, close listening, sight-reading, performance skills
6. First study, instrument or voice (specialist teacher)
7. *Free composition. Portfolio submission*
8. *Dissertation. 4000 words*

---

46 For a useful American perspective on the earlier part of this period, see Hatter (2020).

Second Year courses (II)

Five of the six courses from the 1st year are continued, building on previous work, but there is an additional selected option or two. However, the actual periods and genres of study are now partly at the choice of the student, and this can either represent an opportunity to engage more deeply into a previous area, or cover one that has not yet been touched. The workload is likely to include more substantial written outputs (essays and the like), but dealt with in fortnightly or monthly supervisions, as the student learns to achieve more autonomy over their own educational organization.

1. Harmony, counterpoint, arrangement and orchestration. Portfolio submission
2. Music Analysis. Forms and styles, 19th to 21st century
3. Music History. Two selected periods, genres or styles
4. Practical Music. Conducting, harmonization, figured bass, transposition
5. First study, instrument or voice (specialist teacher)
6. *Free composition. Portfolio submission*
7. *Dissertation. 6000 words*
8. *Notation and editing of music: sources and software skills*
9. *Music Technology*
10. *Second study, instrument or voice (specialist teacher)*

Third Year courses (III)

In the third year, the student focuses more on their specialist areas, with a recommended five courses, only two of which are compulsory. The options selected will depend on the career path in view, and the work moves from typical course- or year-end written examinations to portfolio submissions: the student will need to develop an understanding of how to undertake such year- or term-long tasks and how to create more substantial outcomes. By the end of the three years they should have a solid understanding of what music is, how it works, its history and development, and how it is played, giving them all the skills to start out on a successful career in the field, or undertake further Masters-level study.

1. Music History. One selected period or style
2. First study, instrument or voice (specialist teacher)
3. *Music teaching in theory and practice*

4. *The music business. Copyright, contracts, publicity, freelancing, concert organization, accounting, website design and management, repertoire, agents, working with other musicians, administration, careers, getting published*[47]
5. *Music Analysis. Portfolio submission*
6. *Free composition. Portfolio submission*
7. *Dissertation. 8000 words*
8. *Musical Instruments. Design, history and usage*
9. *Science and music. Acoustics, perception, sound recording*

Examinations

The goal of a course of study, both as a formal end point and a test or evaluation of what has been learned, is still best done by a marked examination of some kind. Historically, for music these could be of four kinds: timed, invigilated written tests; portfolios of agreed pieces of work; practical recitals or other tests; and verbal examination. This last now survives only as an occasional viva voce in the traditional university system, but was actually quite standard until the 19th century, and is worth reviving. The ability to present an argument, and talk coherently about aspects of music and answer questions on it, is an important professional skill.

Each course should have an agreed method of evaluation, and for some components it would be extremely valuable (if an extra cost) to have an external examiner, who could anonymously second-mark written work and provide an additional quality reference point: there is always a potential conflict of interest when formal work is marked only by the teacher who set it. Mark schemes of the precise percentage-type used in some universities are probably not necessary, and a simple pass/fail scheme,[48] with the possibility of an additional Merit or Distinction for work of especially high quality, may both be a sufficient measure of achievement and less stressful for the student.

---

47 These very practical areas related to future careers and employment are often ignored by university courses; however, the new London Performing Academy of Music takes them seriously, under the title of 'Supportive Studies'; see https://www.lpmam.com/supportive-studies.

48 The possibility of retakes, more common in the US than the UK tertiary sector, could be built into the system but can easily become a tempting safety net for the indolent student.

Certification

At the end of a three-year course of this kind, the student would ideally have received about the same quantity and quality of direct-contact teaching as a normal university undergraduate. This will have been at a fraction of the cost, but comes without a formal qualification, which may well be a perceived sticking-point for some students, who study as much to gain a degree as for the education it actually offers. In the absence of external validation for such degrees (and the associated intellectual *imprimatur* that is seen as coming from leading institutions), a private student would be advised as part of their studies to work towards a number of such external music qualifications as are available (see Chapter 5). This begins at the basic level with Associated Board Grade 8 Theory (already accepted as an A-level alternative or supplement to A-level music by many university admissions departments), rising to the various performance and other diplomas offered in relevant instruments by British conservatoires, the Royal College of Organists and others. In addition, some online courses offer completion certificates, and a full study transcript (including course titles, dates, examination dates, results and so on) should also be provided by the Course Director for the entire period of work, in due course enabling potential employers to see what has been covered and when.[49] This matter of certification[50] is especially important for students wishing to proceed to postgraduate study, where diplomas may be considered suitable musical qualifications in the absence of a formal first degree.[51]

---

49 Sechter provided Bruckner with five such certificates for his counterpoint studies; see Hawkshaw (2007), p.116n.

50 A student might also be able to produce some published work, such as an article, either by the end of the course or soon afterwards.

51 Thereafter, a Master's degree may be sufficient to support a PhD application.

5. Diplomas and Higher degrees

Diplomas

At least eight institutions or organizations in Britain alone offer external diplomas in music, both practical and academic, usually graded upwards from Associate to Licentiate to Fellowship. In terms of standard, these might be regarded as the degree equivalent of Bachelor/Bachelor/Master, or sometimes Bachelor/Master/Doctor. They are fee-based, with an examination cost in the hundreds of pounds.[52] Some organizations are longer established and better known than others, but all diplomas require high levels of skill – and in the case of compositions and dissertations, considerable quantity of content. If such qualifications are to form part of the end-point of a course of study, then their requirements should be planned to form the basis of relevant content, for example of performance repertoire, or set works for analysis. Similarly, a period of course-like study just for a single selected diploma, rather than an entire degree, is another possibility.

Masters degrees

The proliferation of Masters courses, both taught and research, over the past few decades is both a reflection of degree inflation – when so many people have a first degree, it can take a second one to set a candidate apart to an employer – and a perception by universities than some specialist courses are relatively straightforward to organize (compared with undergraduate degrees) and are appealing to high-fee-paying overseas students. Courses can last one or two years, and often be taken either full- or part-time. Some are intended as specialist developments of BA subjects, some cross over disciplinary boundaries, some introduce topics not covered at undergraduate level, some have a practical focus, while others are designed to 're-train' students who have moved from other subjects. This level of study for home (UK) students now ranges in per-year fee costs from about the same as undergraduate degree to well above it, with the Open University MA total fee at around two-thirds of the lower sum. There is also the option of completely online courses, as offered by a number of US universities.

---

52 Some offer assessments that can be taken online.

Doctorates

The conventional mode of study is for three full-time years in a residential institution, preferably one where the physical and intellectual resources suitably match the thesis subject; in addition, an expert and supportive PhD supervisor is a primary requirement. The student will expect to work within a small group of peers (regardless of the variety of their own specialisms), at least at the beginning, and to receive formal training in research skills for the first year. Thereafter, the primary intellectual relationship will be with the thesis supervisor, supplemented by conference attendance and occasional consultation with senior scholars in the field. The option of part-time, probably non-residential, study is often an option, with annual fees likely to be half or less than full-time study, although at the cost of a sustained six-year project, which can be a serious challenge for those in full-time jobs or with family responsibilities. The fees are variable between different institutions, but can be in the region of £5,000-10,000 per annum full-time. Overseas residential study is also an option for those with the appropriate language skills, and some countries charge minimal or no fees.

While this long-established PhD 'intellectual apprenticeship' system can work extremely well in optimal conditions, it represents a major further financial commitment for a student. While this is almost certainly a necessity for anyone wishing to enter the formal academic profession, for some others this may instead represent the opportunity for sustained work on a specialized topic, the satisfaction of which may outrank any potential employability or financial gain that a PhD qualification could represent. Obviously, privately writing a book on an equivalent research topic would be an economical alternative, but is likely to prove a serious challenge for a first research project. The support and guidance available within an institution at PhD level is highly beneficial, and it would take some years of experience and maturity for most researchers to be able to work like this at the appropriate level, unaided. There is then is the matter of securing an appropriate academic publisher, to bring the project to completion.

A further option is a doctorate by publication. Previously, these were usually only available to current staff, or to graduates of, an awarding institution; and the work presented might be the kind of heavily research-based book mentioned above, and reflecting a level of achievement and industry equivalent to a 'course' PhD. However, some universities now offer a more external process, by which a student registers (and pays the appropriate fee)[53]

---

53 This might equate to a year's part-time registration. See also Lee (2010).

for a given period (for example, a year), during which they prepare a set of themed and previously published work, with the help of an assigned supervisor, which is submitted together with a substantial explanatory essay tying the works together. This is then examined in a normal and rigorous PhD viva with an external examiner, and awarded only on the basis of it reaching the usual standard of that institution.

This last method requires careful advance planning and preparation, as the candidate will need (unless they already have a large published corpus to select from) to specially create perhaps a dozen thematically-related research articles of the standard to be accepted for publication in suitable peer-reviewed journals. The peer-review process itself functions as a form of precise, usually harsh, supervision (although helpfully some scholars in the field are willing to look over such work privately in advance, where contact has previously been made). This more economical method of study is by no means quick - it would be difficult to produce sufficient work of this kind and quality in less than three years - but it can be undertaken part-time, and the journals' academic validation process itself ought to be a guarantee of the quality of the end product. It not only represents a formal academic doctorate, but means that the candidate would already have a substantial list of publications.

6. Afterword

Although far cheaper than the top Ivy League universities in the US (where annual undergraduate fees can reach nearly $80,000 a year), fee-based university and conservatoire music study in England is under especial pressure both as a degree and career choice in England, as the projected financial rewards and employment stability seem ever more uncertain (indeed, a number of well-established and successful professional musicians have left the field, some permanently, during the recent pandemic). Even compared to other humanities subjects such as English and History, music is vulnerable to the broad economic and cultural changes that are impacting upon universities. New and more flexible ways of studying need to be considered, with a view to lowering financial entry barriers for tertiary level education, in the interest of fairness, accessibility and the long-term survival of the subject itself.

The creation of an alternative way of studying music of the kind described here represents one way forward for individual students, but comes with the significant challenge of correctly identifying three key things: a prospective locally-based Course Director (advice on this might best be sought from retired music academics), a broad area of study; and an understanding of the likely costs. If such a system can be shown to run successfully, it is possible to imagine a private education consultant developing expertise in this area to help potential students get started, as a business model in itself. Similarly, it would be possible to share specific subject syllabuses (see Chapter 4), possibly within a wider network of collaborative teaching, in the same way as can happen with home-schooling.

Students should in no way underestimate the focus and determination that will be needed to see themselves through a demanding long-term programme of individual musical study, but for those unwilling or unable to undertake the traditional undergraduate course model, this can represent a real alternative option, with the potential to create the maximum of educational value at the minimum cost.

Appendix

These lists and links relate to the sample course structure for classical music laid out in Chapter 4; equivalent material can be found for other musical styles and genres. Other comparable diploma schemes can be found in Ireland, Europe, the US and elsewhere.

External music diplomas in the UK

The abbreviations 'C', 'Dip', 'A', 'L', 'AF' and 'F' below represent Colleague, Diploma, Licentiate, Associate Fellowship and Fellow/Fellowship respectively, followed by the acronym of the institution; thus 'ARSM' is 'Associate of the Royal Schools of Music'.

Associated Board, https://gb.abrsm.org/en
> Diplomas in teaching, performance or direction: ARSM, DipABRSM, LRSM and FRSM

Curwen College of Music, https://curwencollegeofmusic.org
> Diplomas by performance or dissertation: DipCCM, ACCM and FCCM

London College of Music, https://www.uwl.ac.uk/study/music
> DipLCM, ALCM, LLCM and FLCM in performance, conducting, composition or by thesis; FLCM in Professional Achievement

National College of Music and Arts, London, https://ncm-london.co.uk
> AFNCollM

North & Midlands School of Music, https://www.nmsm.org.uk
> Performance, composition or dissertation: ANMSM, LNMSM and FNMSM

Royal College of Organists, https://www.rco.org.uk
> Organ performance, teaching and conducting: Certificate of Accredited membership, Choral Directing Diploma, Licentiateship in Teaching, CRCO, ARCO and FRCO

Trinity College London, https://www.trinitycollege.com
> Performance, composition or dissertation: ATCL, LTCL and FTCL

Three Counties School of Music, http://www.threecountiesmusic.co.uk
> Performance or composition diplomas: DipTCSM, ATCSM and FTCSM

Online courses

Many universities and organizations now offer online study courses, which can range from the short and specific to a full degree programme; some are aimed at specific groups, skills or repertoire, such as teachers, music production or music theatre. Prices vary according to the duration of the course. A sample of available courses include:

> Berklee College of Music, https://www.edx.org/school/berkleex

> CityLit, https://www.citylit.ac.uk/courses/performing-arts/music/music-theory-and-musicianship/online

> Coursera, https://www.coursera.org

> Futurelearn, https://www.futurelearn.com

> Harvard University, https://pll.harvard.edu/subject/music

Selected research resources

There are numerous online repositories of scores, books and articles available, both free and subscription access, including the following:

> Choral Public Domain Library, https://www.cpdl.org

> Google Scholar, https://scholar.google.com

> IMSLP, https://imslp.org

> JSTOR, https://www.jstor.org (free read-online access of 100 articles per month, full access via institutional subscription)

pdfdrive, https://www.pdfdrive.com

Refseek, https://www.refseek.com

Répertoire International de Littérature Musicale, https://www.rilm.org

Répertoire International des Sources Musicales, https://rism.info

Some universities and organizations also maintain useful finding lists of content, such as:

https://drm.ccarh.org

https://guides.library.ucla.edu/musicresearch

https://guides.osu.edu/c.php?g=825498&p=5893322

https://libguides.richmond.edu/c.php?g=41817&p=266670

Bibliography

Anicius Manlius Severinus Boethius, *De institutione musica* (Venice, 1491/92).

Thomas Morley, *A plaine and easie introduction to practicall musicke* (London, 1597).

Charles Butler, *The Principles of Musik, in Singing and Setting* (London, 1636).

Christopher Simpson, *A Compendium of Practical Musick* (London, 1667).

William Crotch, *Specimens of Various Styles of Music*, 3 vols. ([1808-1810]).

William Crotch, *Elements of Musical Composition, Comprehending the Rules of Thorough Bass, and the Theory of Tuning* (London, 1812).

John Henry Newman, *The Idea of a University* (1852).

Matthew Arnold, *Culture and Anarchy* (Oxford, 1869).

John Stainer, *The Music of the Bible* (London, 1879).

C. F. Abdy Williams, *A Short Historical Account of the Degrees in Music at Oxford and Cambridge* (London, 1893).

Benjamin Dale, Gordon Jacob and Hugo Anson, *Harmony, Counterpoint & Improvisation* (London, 1940).

Nan Cooke Carpenter, 'The Study of Music at the University of Oxford in the Renaissance (1450-1600)', *The Musical Quarterly*, xli/2 (April 1955), pp.191-214.

John D. Baum, 'Mathematics, Self-Taught', *The American Mathematics Monthly*, lxv/9 (November 1958), pp.701-705.

Mark H. Curtis, *Oxford and Cambridge in Transition 1558-1642* (Oxford, 1959).

Ernst Hess, 'Anton Stadler's "Musick Plan"', *Mozart Jahrbuch* (1962/63), pp.37-54.

James Pruett, 'Charles Butler – Musician, Grammarian, Apiarist', *The Musical Quarterly*, xli/4 (October 1963), pp.498-509.

Charles Cudworth, '500 Years of Music Degrees', *The Musical Times*, cv/1452 (February 1964), pp.98-99.

Thurston Dart, 'The Origins of Music Degrees', *The Musical Times*, cv/1453 (March 1964), pp.190-191.

Jamie Croy Kassler, 'Burney's Sketch of a Plan for a Public Music School', *The Musical Quarterly*, xliii (1972), pp.210-233.

Daniel Heartz, 'Thomas Attwood's Lessons in Composition with Mozart', *Proceedings of the Royal Musical Association*, c (1973-1974), pp.175-183.

Leo Kraft, *Gradus: An integrated approach to harmony, counterpoint, and analysis* (New York, 1976).

András Kárpáti, 'Translation or Compilation? Contributions to the Analysis of Sources of Boethius' De institutione musica', *Studia Musicologica Academiae Scientiarum Hungaricae*, xxix, Fasc. 1/4 (1987), pp.5-33.

Pamela L. Poulin, 'A View of Eighteenth-Century Musical Life and Training: Anton Stadler's "Musick Plan"', *Music & Letters*, lxxi/2 (May 1990), pp.215-224.

Elizabeth Leedham-Green, *A Concise history of the University of Cambridge* (Cambridge, 1996).

Sheldon Rothblatt, *The Modern University and its Discontents: the Fate of Newman's Legacies in Britain and America* (Cambridge, 1997).

Anne Carson, 'The Idea of a University (After John Henry Newman)', *The Threepenny Review*, lxxxviii (Summer, 1999), pp.6-8.

Thomas Benjamin, *The Craft of Tonal Counterpoint* (New York, 2/2003).

Robert Anderson, *British Universities Past and Present* (London, 2006).

Mark Summers, *Analysis of research within unit of assessment 67 (music) of the UK Research Assessment Exercise*, MSc dissertation (Loughborough University, 2007).

Paul Hawkshaw, 'Anton Bruckner's Counterpoint Studies at the Monastery of Saint Florian, 1845-55', *The Musical Quarterly*, xc/1 (Spring 2007), pp.90-122.

Bernarr Rainbow, *Four Centuries of Music Teaching Manuals, 1518-1932* (Woodbridge, 2009).

Alison Lee, 'When the article is the dissertation: Pedagogies for a PhD by publication', in Claire Aitchison, Barbara Kamler and Alison Lee (eds), *Publishing Pedagogies for the Doctorate and Beyond* (London, 2010).

Rosemary Golding, *Music and Academia in Victorian Britain* (Farnham, 2013).

Ronald Hutton, *Pagan Britain* (New Haven, 2013).

Peter Tregear, *Enlightenment or Entitlement: Rethinking Tertiary Music Education* (Sydney, 2014).

Herbert A. Brewer, ed John Morehen, *Memories of Choirs and Cloisters* (London, 2015).

Sam Friedman, Daniel Laurison and Andrew Miles, 'Breaking the "Class" Ceiling? Social Mobility into Britain's Elite Occupations', *The Sociological Review*, lxiii/2 (2015), pp.259-289.

Patricia Shehan Campbell, David Myers and Ed Sarath, 'Transforming Music Study from Its Foundations', *College Music Symposium*, lvi (2016), pp.1-22

Stefan Collini, *Speaking of Universities* (London, 2017).

Noël Riley, *The accomplished lady: a history of genteel pursuits c.1660-1860* (Plymouth, 2017).

Sam Friedman, Dave O'Brien and Daniel Laurison, '"Like Skydiving without a Parachute": How Class Origin Shapes Occupational Trajectories in British Acting', *Sociology*, li/5 (2017), pp.992-1010.

Rosemary Golding, 'Finding Musicology in nineteenth-century Britain: contexts and conflicts', in Melanie Wald-Fuhrmann and Stefan Keym (eds), *Wege zur Musikwissenschaft / Paths to Musicology* (Kassel, 2018).

David Barton, *The autonomy of private instrumental teachers: its effect on valid knowledge construction, curriculum design, and quality of teaching and learning*, PhD thesis, Royal College of Music (London, 2019).

Jack Britton, Lorraine Dearden, Laura van der Erve and Ben Waltmann, 'The impact of undergraduate degrees on lifetime earnings', The Institute for Fiscal Studies (2020), https://www.ifs.org.uk/publications/14729.

Benjamin Rich Zendel and Emily J. Alexander, 'Autodidacticism and Music: Do Self-Taught Musicians Exhibit the Same Auditory Processing Advantages as Formally Trained Musicians?', *Frontiers in Neuroscience* (21 July 2020).

Naomi Bath, Alison Daubney, Duncan Mackrill and Gary Spruce, 'The declining place of music education in schools in England', *Children & Society*, xxxiv/5 (September 2020), pp.443-457.

Jane Hatter, 'Early Music Matters', *College Music Symposium*, lx/2 (Fall 2020), pp.1-13.

Martin Rees, 'Universities must embrace new ways to learn', *The Times* (31 December 2021), p.28.

www.ingramcontent.com/pod-product-compliance
Lightning Source LLC
LaVergne TN
LVHW070839080426
835512LV00025B/3483